KU-709-635

Schools Library and Information Services

S00000663308

KEEPING HEALTHY
Eating

Text by Carol Ballard
Photography by Robert Pickett

HODDER
Wayland

an imprint of Hodder Children's Books

TITLES IN THE KEEPING HEALTHY SERIES:

• Personal Hygiene • Eating • Safety
• Exercise • Relationships • Harmful Substances

© 2004 White-Thomson Publishing Ltd

Produced by White-Thomson Publishing Ltd
2/3 St Andrew's Place, Lewes, BN7 1UP

Editor: Elaine Fuoco-Lang

Consultant: Chris Sculthorpe, East Sussex,
                             Brighton & Hove Healthy
                             School Scheme Co-ordinator

Inside design: Joelle Wheelwright

Cover design: Hodder Wayland

Photographs: Robert Pickett

Proofreader: Alison Cooper

Artwork: Peter Bull

Published in Great Britain in 2004 by Hodder
Wayland, an imprint of Hodder Children's Books.
Hodder Children's Books, a division of
Hodder Headline Limited, 338 Euston Road,
London, NW1 3BH.

The right of Carol Ballard to be identified as the
author of this Work has been asserted by her in
accordance with the Copyright, Designs and Patents
Act 1988.

All rights reserved. No part of this publication may
be reproduced, stored in a retrieval system, or
transmitted, in any form or by any means without
the prior written permission of the publisher, nor be
otherwise circulated in any form of binding or
cover other than that in which it is published and
without a similar condition being imposed on the
subsequent purchaser.

British Library Cataloguing in
Publication Data

Ballard, Carol

Eating - (Keeping Healthy)

1. Diet - Juvenile literature 2. Food - Juvenile
literature

3. Nutrition - Juvenile literature

1. Title

613.2

ISBN 0 7502 4339 2

Printing and binding at C&C China.

Acknowledgements:

The publishers would like to thank the following
for their assistance with this book: the staff and
children at Drapers Mills School, Margate, Kent;
The Mascot Bakery, Herne Bay, Kent; Peter Bull
for all diagrams.

Picture acknowledgements:

Robert Pickett 4 top, 7 bottom, 8, 9 bottom, 11 top, 12
bottom, 14, 15, 16, 17, 18 bottom (left and right), 19,
20, 21 top, 22 bottom, 23 top, 24 bottom, 26, 27, 28
bottom, 29; HWPL 4 bottom, 5, 6, 7 top, 8 bottom, 11
bottom, 12 top, 13, 17 top, 18 top, 21 bottom, 22 top,
23 bottom, 25 top, 28 top.

The photographs in this book are of models
who have granted their permission for their use
in this title.

Contents

DUDLEY PUBLIC LIBRARIES

L   4743

66 3308   SCH

J613.2

Food and water

Every living thing needs food to stay alive. Green plants make their own food using energy from sunlight to produce sugars and starch. Animals cannot do this, so they have to eat plants or other animals. Some animals just eat plants, some just eat other animals, and some eat both plants and animals.

▶ **This tree takes in the energy from the sun through its leaves which helps it to grow.**

Many people have a wide choice of what to eat. Some food is grown locally and some is transported from other countries. Some is fresh and has not been treated with preservatives, while some is produced in factories and packaged so that it will keep for a long time.

◀ **Fresh fruit and vegetables help to keep our bodies healthy.**

Healthy Hints

Water is just as important to us as food – amazingly, humans can survive longer without food than without water! It is important to drink plenty of fresh water, and many doctors suggest we should try to drink 6–8 glasses of water every day. If you cannot get a drink of water easily at school, perhaps you could ask your teachers if they could organize it for you and your classmates.

▲ **Drinking water is very important. We should all aim to drink plenty of water, especially after we exercise.**

◀ **Healthy meals taste great and are good sources of energy for our bodies.**

We need to choose a good balance of foods so that our bodies get all the chemicals that they need to stay healthy, and to grow and repair. Our food must also provide all the energy we need for everyday activities. Some foods are better for us than others – it's up to you to make the best choices!

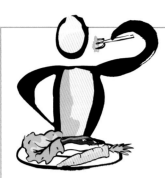

Why do we need food?

We need food for three main things: energy, growth and repair, and staying healthy.

Energy

Everything you do uses energy. Even when you're asleep, your body is still using energy as your heart beats, your lungs breathe and your brain dreams. The more active you are, the more energy you need.

Growth and repair

Your body is made up from millions and millions of tiny building blocks. To grow, more building blocks are needed. When you eat, your body uses food to produce more building blocks.

▲ *When you play judo you are using up lots of energy.*

If you hurt yourself, your body needs to repair the damage. This can be a tiny repair, as in growing new skin to heal a cut, or a bigger repair such as mending a broken bone. All the repairs need the building blocks provided by your food.

Staying healthy

Just as a car needs oil to keep the engine running smoothly, your body needs some things in order to stay healthy. Your food should give your body everything it needs for clear skin, strong teeth and nails, shining hair and for fighting off colds and other illnesses.

▲ *New building blocks are being made to help repair this girl's knee.*

 # Healthy Hints

It's a long time from supper in the evening until lunch the next day, and a good breakfast gives you a much-needed energy boost to start the day. Cereals and milk, bacon and eggs, fruit and yoghurt – there are so many different breakfast ideas there's bound to be one you'll enjoy.

▲ *Choosing a healthy breakfast is good for your body and helps to give you energy you need at the start of the day.*

Too much . . . or too little

Your body is using energy every minute of every day, but some activities use up more energy than others. Sitting on the sofa watching television uses up a lot less energy than having a game of football or going for a ride on your bike. It is important to balance the amount of energy you take in by eating and drinking with the amount of activity you do.

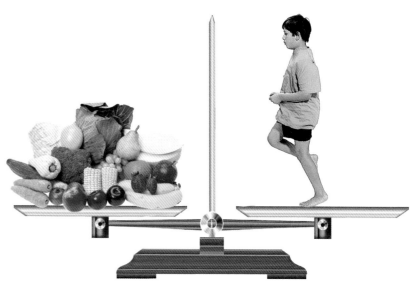

▲ *By eating the right amount of healthy food and exercising you can achieve a perfect balance.*

Too much . . .

If you take in more energy than you use, your body will store the extra energy as fat and you will become overweight. Being very overweight can eventually cause serious health problems, as your heart and lungs have to work harder. It also makes it harder to run and play games and other activities.

◀ *Riding your bike is a great way to exercise.*

Too little . . .

If you take in less energy than you need, your body will start to use up its own energy store and you will lose weight. This might not seem to be much of a problem, but eventually your body will run out of stored energy and will start to use up important parts such as muscles. Being very underweight can make you tired and weak, and causes just as many health problems as being overweight.

► *Not eating enough can cause problems. If you eat healthily and exercise too this will be much better for your body.*

Action Zone

The packaging that many foods comes in gives information about how much energy the food contains. On some packaging find the column that says 'Energy' followed by the number of kilojoules (or kilocalories), the bigger the number, the more energy the food contains. How much energy is in your favourite snack bar?

What do we need?

We can put foods into five main groups, based on what they contain:

- starchy foods such as cereals and bread, pasta and rice
- fruits and vegetables
- meat, fish, eggs, nuts
- dairy products
- fats, oils and sugars

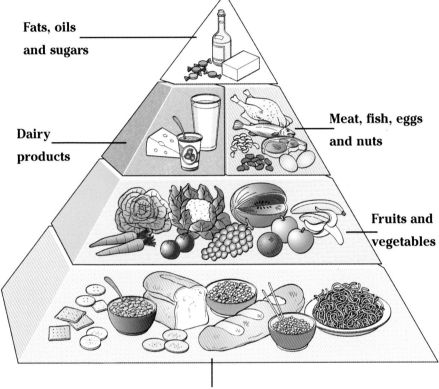

Fats, oils and sugars

Dairy products

Meat, fish, eggs and nuts

Fruits and vegetables

Cereals, bread, pasta and rice

A balanced diet contains something from each of the food groups. If you arrange the food groups into a pyramid, it gives you an idea of the number of helpings of each that many doctors think you should try to eat each day.

At the bottom of the pyramid are the starchy foods. Many nutritionists think that foods such as cereals, bread, pasta and rice should make up the bulk of what we eat.

Fruits and vegetables are important for staying healthy. Five helpings a day is ideal.

▲ *This food pyramid shows the five main food groups.*

10

Action Zone

Whether you had a packed lunch or a school meal today, think about what you ate. Did it have something from each of the five food groups? If it did, well done! If not, perhaps you could make an action plan for yourself to try to make a better choice tomorrow . . . or ask whoever packs your lunch for a piece of fresh fruit every other day. Every tiny change can help you to stay healthier.

► **Having a healthy packed lunch is easy to achieve.**

► **Can you see which food group each food in this meal belongs to?**

Meat, fish, eggs and nuts provide the building blocks for growth and repair. You need to eat some foods from this group, but try not to overdo them.

Dairy products contain many substances that are good for a strong, healthy body but they can also contain a lot of fat too. Again, have some but not too much.

The tip of the pyramid is made up from foods containing fats, sugars and oils. We should think of these as treats – great to enjoy, but not all the time!

Starchy foods

Most starchy foods are made from grains that are the seeds of cereal crops such as wheat, corn, barley, oats and rice. The starch that is in all these foods is a substance called a carbohydrate. It is an excellent source of energy.

Some grains are used whole. Rice can be cooked and used in savoury and sweet dishes. Oats are used to make porridge.

▲ *These starchy foods are all good sources of energy.*

▲ *Pasta is a great source of carbohydrate and there are many different kinds to choose from.*

Some grains are taken to mills where they are ground into flour that can be used to make a wide range of foods, such as bread and pasta. Wholemeal flours, such as those used to make brown bread, contain all the goodness of the grain. White flours have had a lot of the goodness taken out. You might like white bread best – but brown bread is much better for you and will stop you feeling hungry for a lot longer. Why not try making a sandwich with one slice of white and one slice of brown bread? You'll have a bit of what you like plus a bit of extra goodness!

Action Zone

Do you know where different grains come from? Next time you're in a supermarket, have a look at some packets of foods made from grains such as rice, flour, porridge and pasta. Many will tell you which country the grain was grown in. Can you find these countries on a map of the world? Has your food travelled a long way to get to you?

▶ **These women are checking the quality of rice in Italy. Rice is a popular meal in many parts of the world.**

▶ **A tuna sandwich is a really healthy meal – brown bread is better for you than white bread and helps to fill you up.**

It is important to separate plain starchy foods from those that also contain lots of added sugar and fat, such as cakes and biscuits – these may be delicious, but they're definitely in the 'treats' group!

Fruits and vegetables

Raw or uncooked fruits and vegetables are really important as they contain lots of vitamins and minerals. These are substances that our bodies need to stay healthy. Cooking can destroy some vitamins, though, so try to include some fresh fruits and vegetables when you can.

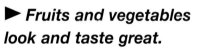

► *Fruits and vegetables look and taste great.*

There are many different types of fruits:

- sharp, tangy citrus fruits like oranges, lemons, grapefruits and tangerines
- peaches, plums and cherries all have a large stone in the middle
- apples and melons have a lot of smaller pips
- strawberries and raspberries have tiny seeds on the outside.

All of the fruits are rich in vitamins and minerals, but those that taste very sweet may have a lot of sugar too.

▼ *Fresh fruit is a healthy snack.*

Different parts of plants are eaten as vegetables:

- leaves, like cabbage, spinach and lettuce

- flowers, like cabbage and broccoli

- stems, like celery

- roots, like carrots, turnips and parsnips

- fruits of the plants like beans, peas, sweetcorn, tomatoes and cucumbers.

Vegetables are also full of vitamins and minerals, but usually contain less sugar than fruits.

▶ Raw vegetables such as celery or a carrot make a handy snack which is full of vitamins.

\?/ Fantastic Facts

When sailors spent many months at sea in sailing ships, it was impossible to keep a supply of fresh food aboard. All the men had to eat were dry biscuits and salted meat. Many died of a disease called scurvy. At last, an English doctor found that lime juice could prevent scurvy. English ships began to carry supplies of limes and lime juice, and English sailors became known as 'limeys'. Later, scientists discovered that limes, like many other citrus fruits, contain a lot of vitamin C, and this is what prevented scurvy.

Fruits and vegetables also provide fibre. This is plant material that our bodies cannot absorb and use. It is important, though, as it helps the digestive system to work smoothly, and ensures that food keeps moving along the intestines.

Meat, fish, eggs and nuts

Foods such as meat, fish, eggs and nuts provide proteins. These are the building blocks from which much of our bodies are made. We need proteins to grow, to repair damage and for strength.

There are many ways in which you can include protein foods in your diet. Hot meals can include meats such as roast chicken, steak and pork chops. Meat can be processed to make other products such as sausages and beefburgers. Some meat such as ham is eaten cold in salads and sandwiches.

Fried fish and chips are delicious, but try some other ways of eating fish too. These are just as tasty and much better for you as they contain less fat than fried fish. How about a piece of fish like salmon cooked in the oven, or haddock made into tasty fish cakes?

▼ *Grilling fish is a healthy alternative to frying.*

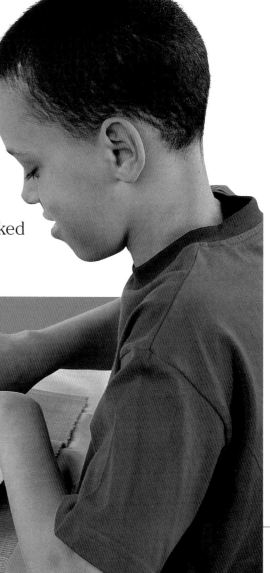

Eggs are full of proteins too, and there are lots of ways to enjoy them – soft-boiled, hard-boiled, poached, scrambled, in an omelette – which is your favourite?

◀ *Many people enjoy a protein-packed breakfast.*

 # Healthy Hints

It's a good idea to include some protein food in your diet every day. This might be meat, fish, eggs or nuts. You might have bacon for breakfast, or chicken nuggets for lunch, or cheese omelette for dinner. What would you choose as your favourite protein food for tea? What protein foods could you put in a packed lunch ?

▲ *You might love a fried breakfast but try not to have this too often. Brown toast or cereals that are low in sugar are far better for you.*

Milk products

Milk provides us with a lot of different nutrients, including proteins, fats, vitamins and minerals. It is rich in calcium, which helps to build strong teeth and bones.

Most of our milk comes from cows, but you can also get milk from sheep and goats. Our milk is usually pasteurised; this means it has been heated to kill any microbes that may harm us. Some or all of the fat may be skimmed off, to give semi-skimmed or skimmed milk.

▲ *A glass of delicious ice-cold milk is a really healthy drink.*

►*Cow's milk is very popular.*

►*You can try goat's milk for a change.*

Cold milk is great as a drink on its own, but you can add flavourings to it and whisk it up to make tasty milk shakes. Hot milk is good in hot chocolate drinks, and it makes delicious custards and other puddings.

Milk is used to make many other foods. It can be churned to make butter and cheese. Yoghurt is made from milk, that has been soured by adding special microbes. Fruits and flavourings are added to give a wide variety of different tastes.

◄ *Cheese, butter and yoghurt are all made from milk.*

!?/ Fantastic Facts

We usually think of bacteria as being germs and therefore bad for us, but cheeses and yoghurts are made by adding bacteria to milk. The bacteria feed on the sugars in milk and produce an acid, which gives cheeses and yoghurts their distinctive sour tastes. Different types of bacteria are used to produce a range of different tastes.

► *Bacteria give yoghurts their sharp, tangy taste.*

Sugars, fats and oils

Energy is needed for all the things that we do every day. From sitting still and reading a book to running around playing tennis, everything we do needs energy.

Sugars, fats and oils are important energy sources for our bodies. Any energy that you eat and don't use is stored as fat, so you need to maintain a balance between what you eat and what you use.

▼ *Sugary foods taste great but you shouldn't eat them too often.*

Sugary foods like sweets, cakes and biscuits are sweet – and most people think they're delicious. Foods rich in fats like chips, other fried foods and crisps are often really tasty too. Some, like jam doughnuts, are full of fat and sugars. We all have our favourite sugary and fatty foods, but we should try to think of them as treats – it's fine to have them now and again, but best not to have them every day.

▶ *Try not to eat too many fatty snacks like these crisps.*

 # Healthy Hints

There is a strong link between eating lots of sugary foods and drinking sugary drinks and tooth decay. Bacteria in the mouth feed on the sugar and produce acid. This slowly eats into the teeth, making a hole called a cavity. Avoiding eating sweets between meals can help to reduce tooth decay.

▶ *Eating fresh fruit instead of sweets as a snack is not only better for your body, but it is better for your teeth.*

Being vegetarian or vegan

Vegetarians are people who do not eat meat or fish. Some choose to be vegetarian because they do not like the idea of animals being used for food. Some think there may be health risks with particular types of meat. Some are vegetarian for religious reasons.

▲ *A jacket potato with a cheese topping is a great vegetarian alternative to tuna or ham.*

Vegans avoid all animal products, so as well as avoiding meat and fish they do not eat any eggs or milk products.

◄ *These nuts and pulses are all great sources of protein.*

!?/ Fantastic Facts

Most people with a vegetarian in the family are concerned to know that they are getting enough proteins, but other nutrients are important too and are often forgotten about. Vegetarians need to make sure that they eat plenty of whole grains and cereals which are rich in B vitamins. These are a very important group of vitamins, which keep many different parts of the body healthy.

▶ Wholegrains and cereals are rich in B vitamins which are important for vegetarians and vegans.

The most important thing about being vegetarian or vegan is to eat a balanced diet, just as you should if you eat meat or fish. Many foods from plants such as nuts, beans and lentils contain proteins and so some vegetarians eat these instead of meat. Many manufactured meat-substitutes are also available now, including foods made from soya beans. Milk made from soya beans can be used instead of animals' milk.

◀ Pasta with a tomato sauce and cheese is a quick, easy and healthy vegetarian option.

Fast food

Fast food is exactly what its name says – food that takes very little time to be ready to eat. Fast foods suit our increasingly busy lifestyle, when many people are trying to cram more and more into every day. It can be difficult to find time to prepare a meal starting with fresh ingredients and, once prepared, there may still be a long cooking time. So, many people turn to the quick and easy alternative – fast food, bought either in a packet at the supermarket, or from a take-away restaurant.

▲ *Eating a beefburger is fine, as long as you don't eat them too often.*

Fast food can be fashionable. Some manufacturers sell their product to appeal especially to children and young people – have you ever pestered your parents to take you to a place where there's a free toy on offer?

◀ *Burger and chips made at home are often more healthy than from a fast-food restaurant.*

Fast food can be tasty and it certainly takes the work out of preparing a meal – but there are snags too. Some fast foods are of excellent quality, but others contain poor-quality ingredients. Processing the food can destroy vitamins and other nutrients. Many fast foods contain very high levels of fats, sugars and salt.

Healthy Hints

Most people eat fast foods sometimes, perhaps chips for a quick lunch or a take-away pizza for dinner. That's absolutely fine – there is no harm in enjoying these foods occasionally, as long as you try to eat plenty of fresh food as well. Fast foods definitely belong in the 'treats' group.

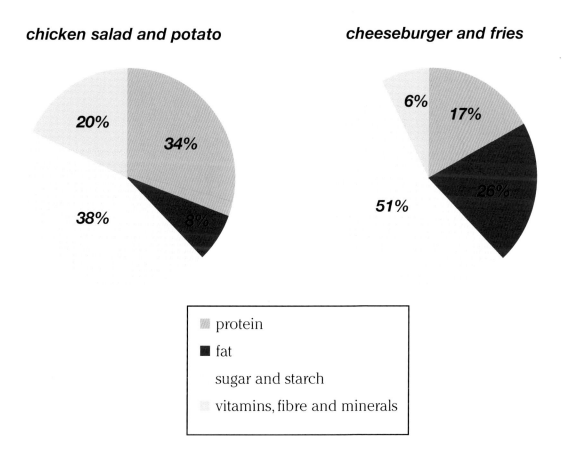

chicken salad and potato

20%

34%

38%

8%

cheeseburger and fries

6%

17%

51%

26%

- protein
- fat
- sugar and starch
- vitamins, fibre and minerals

▲ *This diagram shows the different nutritional content of two meals.*

Preparing food

Food that is not clean, or that has not been prepared properly, can make us ill. By following a few basic food hygiene rules, you can make sure that the food you prepare is clean and good to eat.

Everything that food touches should be clean. This includes anything it is wrapped in, the container it is put in, the work surface on which it is prepared, and utensils such as knives and spoons. And don't forget yourself – remember to wash your hands before you touch food.

▲ *Head scarves are used to keep hair away from the bread and cakes at this bakery.*

Check any cooking instructions carefully. Food that is just warm and not cooked properly can cause sickness and tummy ache. This is especially important when you're using a microwave oven, as food can be hot around the edges and still cold in the middle.

Once your meal is prepared, make sure the work space is clean and tidy ready for the next meal. Microbes can grow on scraps of food, so wash any utensils you have used and wipe the work surfaces.

◀ *Your kitchen should be as clean and tidy as this one.*

Action Zone

Next time you prepare food, even if it's only a sandwich, check each of these off in your head:

- Have I washed my hands?
- Is the work surface clean?
- Have I got a clean plate or dish?
- Are my utensils clean?
- Have I checked the 'use by?' date (see page 29) on the food?
- Have I left the kitchen clean and tidy?

▲ *Make sure that you wash your hands before preparing food.*

Storing food

We say food is 'going off' or has 'gone bad' when it is no longer at its best. Some foods go off very quickly, others keep for a much longer time.

Breads, fresh meats, dairy products, fruits and vegetables start to decay as microbes grow on them, making them discoloured and often smelly.

◀ **Fruit can go mouldy quite quickly.**

Microbes need three things to grow – warmth, moisture and food. If we take away any one of these, the microbes cannot grow. We can remove warmth by keeping foods in a cold place such as a fridge. This is a good way of storing meat, fish and dairy products. Many types of food can be kept for a long time in a freezer. We can remove the moisture by drying the food and sealing it in a container. This is a good way of storing foods such as pasta, rice and lentils.

▶ **The cold temperature in the fridge helps to keep food fresh.**

▲ *The meat in this picture will go off quickly if it isn't kept cool.*

Salt kills microbes, and for hundreds of years people have stored foods such as meat in salt. Microbes can be killed by acids, such as the vinegar used for making pickles and chutneys. High temperatures kill microbes too, and so many foods are heated before they are sealed into cans and bottles.

 # Healthy Hints

Most food packets and containers have a date marked on them saying 'use by' or 'best before'. These are to help you to make sure that the food you eat is always good and not going off. It makes good sense to check before you eat, especially on foods like yoghurts that only stay fresh for a few days.

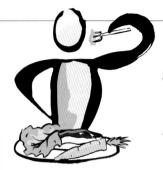

Glossary

bacteria a type of microbe. Some bacteria can be used to make cheese and yoghurt.

balanced diet foods that contain all the nutrients that your body needs.

calcium a mineral that helps to build strong teeth and bones.

carbohydrate a type of nutrient that is a good source of energy.

diet everything you eat and drink.

digestive system the parts of your body that take the goodness out of your food.

fat a type of nutrient that is a good source of energy.

fibre a substance in fruits and vegetables that helps the digestive system to work properly.

hygiene keeping clean and healthy.

intestines part of the digestive system.

kilojoules (kilocalories) a measure of the amount of energy a food contains.

microbe a living thing that is too small to be seen without a microscope.

minerals substances that your body needs to stay healthy.

nutrients the parts of your food that your body can use.

pasteurise to kill microbes by heating.

protein a nutrient that is needed for growth and repair.

scurvy a disease caused by lack of vitamin C.

starch a type of carbohydrate.

vegan a person who does not eat any animal products.

vegetarian a person who does not eat meat.

vitamins substances that your body needs to stay healthy.

Other books to read

Your Food by Claire Llewellyn (Franklin Watts 2002)

Good Enough To Eat by Lizzy Rockwell (HarperCollins, 1999)

Eating – My Healthy Body series by Veronica Ross (Belitha Press, 2002)

Why Do I Vomit? by Angela Royston (Heinemann Library, 2003)

Why Should I Eat This Carrot and other questions by Louise Spilbury (Heinemann 2003)

Useful addresses

For information on healthy eating contact:-

British Nutrition Foundation

High Holborn House

52-54 High Holborn

London

WC1V 6RQ

Tel: 020 7404 6504

Fax: 020 7404 6747

email postbox@nutrition.org.uk

The British Dietetic Association

5th Floor, Charles House

148/9 Great Charles Street Queensway

Birmingham

B3 3HT

Tel: 0121 200 8080

Fax: 0121 200 8081

email info@bda.uk.com

Index